NO SENSE OF GRANDEUR

Margar(

GW01081551

Typeset and Published
by
The National Poetry Foundation
(Reg Charity No 283032)
27 Mill Road
Fareham
Hants PO16 0TH
(Tel: 0329 822218)

Printed by
Meon Valley Printers
Bishops Waltham (0489 895460)

Sponsored by Rosemary Arthur

Cover Photograph by Celia Rambaut

For Jennie, Peter and Tom.

Poems in this book have also appeared in: *Poet's England (Kent), Pause, Outposts, Envoi, Vision On (Ver Poets), Ver Poets' Voices, Iota, Poetry Nottingham* and *New Spokes*.

Previous publication: *'Keeping Company'*, NPF 1989.

ISBN 1 870556 12 7

CONTENTS

PARTY FARE

It was a stocking and gloves occasion,
I had to eat cake with a fork
and be informed about art.

"No, we don't have hobbies – we travel
a bit and there is the DIY and we go
to most of the exhibitions don't we dear
(we, we miss only very few). We have
a married daughter down in Chichester..."
(that's right, I'd know from her demeanour
that she hadn't a son in Katmandu)...

"I tell him – you must walk faster – I
always walk very fast to keep myself fit..."

"They were very young but it's turned out
very well – they are a nice family – like
ours – the right background you know
and the same *standards*..."

I edged away in search of greener thought
– perhaps to meet the sculptress by the door,
water diviner, homespun, in the corner,
or even my agéd friend with the melodious
voice, lest I should die of suffocation.

"Just half a glass thank you...
No more nuts."

FROG TIME

Always when first the wind blew
they'd come. It was an early Spring
that year and when I cleaned the pond
they had arrived – just four of them –
one pair – two singles.

I sat them on the bank – apologised.
They looked resentful – muddy.
The fish had preferential treatment
swimming golden in their bowl.

The frogs kept plopping back
and I returned them to the edge.
I never thought they wouldn't wait
but when the pond was filled again,
the pondweed rinsed and lilies trimmed
they'd gone – back to the log pile
and the half flat stones or hollow bricks
as if they had been wrong about the Spring.

And I felt chastened, cruel.
I asked a friend to give me spawn
in the event they never should return.
I took no joy seeing the crystal water
and the lonely fish – my frogs were gone.

Then two weeks later from the window
I saw the surface was disturbed,
went out and heard the croaking
before they hid at my approach.
I noticed they had spawned:
I was forgiven.

NETTING SWIFTS

Above the watercress-trimmed mirror of the stream
the swifts dive, dart and plane away, follow
the dancing gnats. Black arcs against the apricot
late evening sky they scream in hurtling crescentic
swoops. The night wind sighs in the sallows.

Confused by too many reflections
they skim headlong into the treacherous net
which spans the river. The sleek and lovely wings
are trapped, ruffled by dark tarred string
as struggling they get the more enmeshed.

Bird-lovers lift them gently from the net
soothing their panic, but though they have
no thought to harm or kill, the fear in those
black eyes is much the same. The leg is ringed;
researchers claim it doesn't hurt the bird
and yet their freedom is impaired. Who knows
how much they fret such a loss?

VAN GOGH'S IVY

(The Van Gogh brothers were buried in Auvers, their graves covered with ivy. On the wall behind is a simple plaque which states: "Ivy as a symbol of constant affection links Theo's and Vincent's graves, two brothers who loved each other tenderly").

After much searching it was in Monmartre
that Vincent found a room. "I know you'd like it,
it is small," he wrote, "but overlooks
a garden full of ivy and wild vines."

Teaching in London he could feast his eyes
on "Hampton Court, it's avenues of lime trees,
noisy with rookeries, and Whitehall overgrown
with ivy at the back." From Syon Park
he saw "far off the lights of Isleworth,
its church with ivy," and again when back
in Holland says his lodgings, "overlooked
old houses clad with ivy," quotes his beloved
Dickens: "A strange plant is the ivy green."

Even his sister's pictures he describes
as "framed in ivy." This consistent passion
spurred him to paint one of his greatest works,
light from behind the trees covered with ivy,
streaming golden, brilliant, lighting only
the leaves which turned towards its radiance leaving
the rest in deep green shadow.

So at the last by some enlightened chance,
or could it be design, the ivy clothes
his grave and Theo lies beside him, he
who lost all purpose when his brother died,
oblivious of the needs of wife and child,
as if those creeping stems which bind the graves
were clutching at his soul while he yet lived.

GALE FORCE

He roars for more, only pausing to take breath,
lord of the weather driving out timid drizzle
or sighing summer breeze. King of the elements
he fans the flames of fires, harasses the demented
air and chasms up the smooth reflecting sea
into a howling cauldron, calls all things
to his fury.

The forge glows white, the stricken clouds
are torn, frayed out across the sky; branches
clatter, snap and fall and still he screams
for more. Crofters know better than to check
him, for leashed he'll take the roof off
in his stride.

The unlatched fanlight bangs, smoke billows
into the sitting room, smells cottagey.
Sheets tear at the line and sleet drives level;
rooks fly haphazard, flung to his fancy,
and the driven leaves rustle in dusty corners.

Next day dawns blue, serene as if a dream
had vanished with the light – even the debris
of tiles and branches now seems innocent
devoid of last night's anger.

"The snow is pure and fragile,"
he wrote, echoing Francis Thompson
though he could not know.

"Happiness," wrote his brother,
"happiness is when Mummy cooks the dinner.
Happiness is when the class is quiet."

Nobody told him that he must
be cynical and if possible
a little vulgar. No one said
beauty was old hat and a bit naïve
and sentimental –

or "there are other trees than willows
you know and everyone has already
written about Spring and Death and
Chernobyl and cow parsley and wood pigeons...

You don't think of beauty
if you live in the harsh north–east,
you've got your blinkers off.

Life is real: life is ugly."

DREAM WANDERER

(In the forests of Borneo, Lorne and Lawrence Blair sought out the nomadic Punans hitherto believed to be extinct).

"It's difficult," the pilot said.
"Air–strips can come and go in the encroaching
jungle: rescue's perforce uncertain."
We said we'd take our chance, determined
we should find the nomad Punans.
"Only old Bereyo, the hunter of rhinoceros
would know, " they said, "he's tracked there
for a lifetime, but it means a six day journey
and he might be walkabout."

We travelled through uncharted forest, asking
for help, cajoling, paying our debts
with salt; through unremitting canopy,
over the green and greasy rivers,
single file through knotted jungle
tormented by leeches, and the ants
which in great glistening rivers inches
deep, appeared and vanished.

Bereyo consented, and with replenished stores
of venison and rice we journeyed on,
poling our way upstream against the boiling current,
twenty more days in claustrophobic jungle
avoiding poisonous shrubs, dangerous
when disturbed, thread leeches that invade
the nostrils, mouth and lungs.

When rice and venison ran out we lived
on poison-darted monkey, lizard and bamboo.
Bereyo psycho-navigated with his vision
and with lucid dream. No stars could
guide us, we were divorced from sun
and sky by that vast canopy, only
dream wanderer could guide us on.

"We Punans have two souls," he said,
"one here," smacking his forehead with his palm,
"and one dream wanderer who travels on in dream
and special trance, sees things with different eyes,
pathways of animals and lost tribes."
On we trudged coming upon great waterfalls
and soaring cliffs lost in the jungle's heart.
Then came the rains, the air grew dark, asphyxiating,
but he could see the Punans, clear in his mind's eye
half a day's journey down the swollen river,
there in a longhouse sitting out the storm.

So the dream wanderer led us on and Bereyo had no doubt
but we had no such certainty – bred in more brittle lands,
our extra senses stifled perhaps by noise and rush and
                                        smoke.
We sent scouts down the river to see if it were true.
The watery sun, more like a moon, peered at us in our
                                        clearing
as we waited. Insects invaded sucking our blood and
sweat.

9

The scouts returned – dream wanderer was right,
his guess substantiated and his second sight.
Perched in precarious canoes we thundered down
to hidden fairyland, cathedrals of branches
interlaced over the broadening river, and the sound
of Punan music. Young girls waist deep in water
cupped their hands, beating the surface with
their special rhythm, and then the longhouse
and the cry: "They're here!"

DRESS SENSE

You should have had more glitter
on your Caribbean cruise, you told us,
and more stylish shoes to match the clientele.
My friend, amused, said:
"Don't bring your sequins up to Shrewsbury."

You may need something smart
in a West End London street
with your artistes' club and concerts
and bright lights or when you take
the stage to play or sing – but
don't take your sequins up to Shrewsbury.

When you're tramping the Long Mynd
in an unforgiving wind
or laden down with shopping on the bus
you're better with strong shoes,
a storm–proof mac and old rucksack,
so don't take your sequins up to Shrewbury.

CURLEW

He went, like all the others, willing, brave,
restrained about the fears he must have felt...
"but if I don't come back you'll hear me
in the curlew's cry," he said. Now always
he is there among his native hills as that
wild bird warms to its song, louder and faster,
becoming urgent, those plaintive notes which
sharpen up the morning in early light with
the blown mist and dewdrops on the heather.

Perhaps he's hidden in the next fold of hills,
striding the moors in the high blue morning
and the singing wind and where the copper-bellied
dipper flies through the waterfall, or stretched
out on a flat rock midstream, basking in mellow
sunshine, dreaming and timeless, while the bird
changes its note to a soft bubbling among
the sun-drenched hills in long hot afternoons.

His family mourned the lost promise of his early
youth, the broken beauty of his glowing limbs,
and all the utter waste of war. Spring came
unheeded while his parents wept – what use
the old stone manor house, his home, the lake
with boat tied to the willow tree, the fragrance
of narcissus in the wind, for heartbreak overwhelmed
it all. Now the bitterness has gone, the anguish
fades and the eternal beauty of the moors lives on.

He has not changed from that fair winsome boy
untainted by the infection of rush and stress
in dismal dusty towns, nor plagued by doubt and fear,
young and unfettered as those wild birds.
Watch for him then crossing the packhorse bridge
that spans the upper reaches of the river,
climbing a limestone wall or leaning on a gate
as daylight fades or, as the tide ebbs, wading
along the estuary at twilight.

The bird is silent, the silver loneliness
of moonlight spreads her veiled magic across
the sleeping land and beauty has outwitted death.

THE MERCER FROM TENTERDEN

He would retire, follow his interest
in that engrossing art he'd learnt in Bruges.
Eagerness lit his mind for now
even the richest in their gracious homes
had libraries of only thirty books
copied laboriously. His vision leapt,
foresaw how everybody could enjoy,
possess, the printed word. His voice
as author and translator should extend
to homes throughout the land.

He would print Chaucer's *'Canterbury Tales'*,
the stories set in his beloved Kent,
Malory's *'Morte d'Arthur'*, *'Golden Legend'*,
chess instructions and *'Reynart the Foxe'*,
'The Myrrour of the World' enhanced with woodcuts...
he would be cautious, printing out small pieces,
romances that would sell and which would pay
for works which were religious or austere.

He wouldn't print the Bible, that could start
men thinking for themselves. Lollards explaining
Scripture in the native tongue were burnt
as heretics. It was too dangerous
to be involved.

He would need metal alloy soft enough
to trim up with a chisel, type and paper
from abroad and on his books he'd write
"Thus have I learned and practyssed my grete charge
and dispense to ordeyne said book in prynte."

Wars of the Roses came and went. Meanwhile
the peaceful revolution had begun,
there in a London street beside the Abbey.
Its influence and magic would not die
though books be censored, burned, nothing would stem
the surge of this inimitable power.
Knowledge and records now would be in print
instead of memory and its helpmate, song.
The prince he'd known in Holland, now the King,
gave him his patronage, underwrote his courage.

It all began when Edward, the old King,
brought Flemish families to live in Kent
and manufacture cloth. "Why send the wool
to Flanders, we can weave it here," he said.
They were hard days – men lived on "rye and barly,
benes and peses, well were hym that myghte
thereeof have near ynowe." Those who complained
had their heads rot on poles on London Bridge.
He'd lived in Bruges till he was fifty–four,
returned with a more precious freight than even
his richest fellow merchants ever dreamt of.
Borne by enthusiasm to his seventieth year
he died, his last translation "fynysshed
at the laste days of hys lyffe –

> wyllyam Caxton of westmestre
> MCCCLxxxxi

15

THE INJURED TREE

I cried when they asked us
to mutilate the tree.
Could it be cut, they said.

I thought they wanted cuttings
that they also could possess
its golden glory. But no,
they grudged its swaying
in the wind. It rubbed the
bricks they said. He said
he was too old to keep
repairing bloody bricks.
Well, soon in any case it
will be dead, they said,
rubbing its bark like that.

We don't have many hurricanes,
I said – (but not to them).

We lopped the top – good neighbours
and cruel butchers.
Perhaps it will
bush out and good come out of bad,
we said. But all that golden crown
of flowers which dared to grow too high
is gone. The poet's *'aspens dear'*
were not more loved or mourned
than my poor, wounded golden blossom tree.

WENDY'S HOUSE

It could have been a hearthrug folded
beneath the chair in that old rambly house,
but when she said "it's deaf, be careful"
I had to look again. It sighed, lifted its head
and sniffed, then with resignation pushed its nose forward
on its hairy paws and slept; from time to time
opened its eyes to look through the fringed curtain
at table legs and shadows, sunlight through the door,
a tool case and some slates, a piece of rope,
and two black labradors that padded to and fro.

It roused itself, took a short walk,
turned round to flatten the imagined grass,
grunted and fell once more to sleep.
All was still – only the sound of traffic.
The wet nose twitched as if it sensed
not only dust and distant smell of people
but all that vivid world of chase and kill,
the warm blood spurting as it sank its teeth,
its kin sharing the carcase, body's comfort,
sleeping beneath the moon in a far country.

FRENCH FARM IN WARTIME

Beyond the worn stone steps the flickering fire
lit up the rugged faces as they mused.
The old man dreamed, smoking his favourite brier,
his mind had grown disordered and confused
sitting beside the ancient kitchen range.
Part of the house had long since been disused
and he had witnessed every kind of change
since coming to the farm when still a boy
when everything had been so new and strange,
awaking as he had to each new joy
about the farm, the cattle and the wheat,
which now the Germans threatened to destroy.

He looked around from his snug chimney seat
remembering the farm in far-off days
and felt the bitterness of this defeat.
His children bore him up in countless ways
since that cruel year in which his wife had died;
he watched their faces in the fireside blaze,
the family he loved and on which he relied.
The cold wind howled and draughts blew through the door,
a child upstairs stirred in its sleep and cried,
the sheepdog stretched out on the flagstone floor.

He thought about his grandson, he the one
who was so good with horses, who before
he went to war sung songs that none
could ever quite forget – their magic power
to speed long winter evenings when the sun
set in mid–afternoon, and at this hour
he would grow restless and his thoughts would turn
to think of him, so many hopes gone sour,
his favourite who he prayed would soon return
unharmed, as if his thus believing so
would bring him home. He thought he could discern
his face among the shadows, just as though
he'd come in from the farm in the night air
with eager bearing and bright eyes aglow.

*(Based on Patrick Garland's
novel "The Wings of the Morning.")*

19

SUPERMARKET

After a lifetime in a high-powered
job he ends up trailing his wife
around the supermarket.

She gossips with her friends –
"Murder in here this morning
and so many down with flu,
Angela's bad with it, and three
children to look after..."

"Look Bill – that might be nice."
Women are browsers – they like
to ponder and to take their time.

The wayward trollies bump
and cut the ankles – the old
ones are more wilful than the new;
they twist the back – perhaps
the trolley-makers do a deal
with orthopaedic surgeons.

One man queued three times to pay.
Each till put "This position closed"
at his approach. He wrenched the trolley,
overturned the lot. "Keep your bloody stuff"
he said.

The small shops carry their own
special brand of aggro – they don't
have blanks to duplicate that key –
it's out of date – the manager is out –
no, only at Christmas, no, not
in your size Madam.

UNPOSTED LETTER

Dear Les,

It's no good writing you a letter.
Children send letters up the chimney
addressed to Santa Claus, but we outgrew all that.
The heavy veil is thick as carpet,
dark as a smoggy night
and all the lines are down.

Yet that evening in the garden
I heard your voice. There
as I knelt weeding nasturtiums,
sad yet peaceful. Was it my need
which forced the bolted door?
"Hello," you said, warmly but breathless
as if you couldn't stay. Astonished
I made sure that no one was about
and I was not mistaken, yet
there was no need – your voice and all
its dear inflections, the voice I'd always known
was proof enough it was no dream.

WENDOVER DEAN

Among the dandelions in open fields
there was time to watch the clouds crowd up and break
and mass again, time to watch petals move
and on an island in the river see
a moorhen chip its egg, emerge bedraggled.

We rode the horses bareback through the woods,
jeered at the fate of Absalom, ran through
the farm free as the timeless day. We taught
a calf to butt, pushing the curly forehead,
matching his strength, found kittens among straw
still blind, with ears too small to look like cats,
and in the lane white bryony laced the hedges
and glow-worms lit the ditch at sundown.

One morning in the listening dawn I walked
to Lee through unfamiliar fields
up the beckoning track bordered with violets
to find the village hidden in the mist,
dew on the grass. I stood there spellbound
as the cockerel crowed, greeting the rising sun,
his iridescent feathers shining green and ochre
with no one else awake as if we shared a secret.

In noonday heat we watched the blacksmith
shoe the horses, bellows brightening up the fire
with ringing anvil and the smell of scorching hair.
In winter we went chumping, dragging logs
set on a sledge of branches, rustling down
the hanging woods, the orange sun shining
through coppiced hornbeams
with autumn smell of beech leaves
and pheasants calling in the dusk. We ran unfettered,
free and untidy as the tangled wood
and by the cottage hearth put the huge logs
across the iron basket, sparks flying as they burnt
through and fell, with pungent smell of wood smoke.
In spring we gathered strawberries, among
the primroses and moss south of the larch wood.
There were no yesterdays and no tomorrows.

MOTH AND RUST

Eating through the woolly jumper
left forgotten in the drawer
we are quite a thriving party
and of course there will be more.

Mealy maggots, pale pupae,
full-grown adults in their pairs
look for wider grubbier pastures
try the carpet on the stairs.

We can teach mankind the lesson
written in the ancient book,
lay your treasure up in heaven,
never cast a backward look.

With our metal-working partner
where the broken girders rust
we will concentrate on fabrics
see that they are turned to dust.

RENEWAL

When I think of lowering northern skies
and the bite of the fresh wind across
the sea loch as we took the ferry
through gleaming level rays which lit
the water, rinsed cottages
to radiant white against the ancient pines,
I forget the smoke and traffic
of the Finchley Road, the crowded underground
and jaded, sleepy people, fettered by fear
with tired eyes and stagnant blood.

I will return and know again
the smell of seaweed, feel of bare feet
on turf and sound of summer laughter.

LLANTHONY ABBEY

They ate their sandwiches
sitting against the ruined walls,
they didn't see men in brown habits
kneeling in the nave.
They brought out beer and wine
on cheap tin trays, greeted
their boisterous friends.
They didn't hear the distant
sound of plainsong or see the light
shine through the clerestory
on to the mosaic chancel floor
or sense, amid tobacco fumes,
the incense rising to the shadowed beams.

But when they'd all departed,
as dusk descended and the night
wind stirred the watching trees,
only then soft footsteps could be heard,
cowled figures moved among the arches'
lengthening shadows with sandalled tread
on the dew–softened turf, driven
by a compulsion to return, through wind
and weather or through sweltering heat,
through years of peace and times of war.

Fugitive the suspended moment
hangs in the trembling air.
One breath and they are gone.
Only the river catches the rhythm
and murmurs of what has been
across the echoing meadow.
The ancient walls stand stark and mute
as cold or summer heat
bite at their crumbling feet.

"Have a nice day," they said –
independently, though they knew
it was hot summer weather
and that I must say goodbye
to my good friend – "Have a nice
day"! In all that dust and noise?
Everyone rushing to cool their cars,
get home quickly, overtaking,
arrogant or with aplomb, making it
clear you're an idiot going so slowly.

Moving from blazing sunshine
into a tunnel I saw two girls
walking towards me on the road.
I slowed. "Run out of petrol
Grandma have you?" they shouted out.
("Have a nice day," they'd said).

Is it the lure of *any* journey
or because your neighbour's plot
is always greener? Mid hoots,
loud bangs and screeches, poisonous fumes,
well–wishers safe and cool in flowered gardens
I returned.

"Glad you had a nice day,"
they said.

LILY POND

Often I remember that sun-baked corner
of the garden, secret, safe and mine.
It was a walled-in bowl with prickly mesh of hollies
holding back the boisterous wind.
One side was open to the downs and distant sea
yet the smell of sea-wrack and tarred wood
borne on the salt wind only hinted of a world outside.

I was alone with the deep reflecting pool,
the fish blowing bubbles, slithering through weed,
eating from my hand, and tiny frogs hopping
on the lily pads – silence save for the pine cones
cracking open in the heat. Mauve thyme covered
the rocks and scented the air as I crushed it.
Blue thistles grew as tall as I was
and evening primroses shone in the twilight.

Every summer we unearthed the tap beneath
a stone to turn the fountain, brushing the brass wings
free of chalky soil, ran through the rainbow spray.

We all loved that place, but its richest wonders
would be withheld until I was alone – then I might
see a grass snake or a pigmy shrew, hold my breath,
hear only my own blood pulsing in my ears,
alone in the listening air.

It is a path for courting couples
or those with plastic hips –
a staid and stuffy stifled path
so safe and dull that all the bores
of all the country round are there
– respectable – taking the air.
"The lake is pretty isn't it."

They walk in tailored skirts
and polished shoes, their clothes
are neat and almost new, correct,
the scene only redeemed by two
wet Bernese mountain dogs.

Above them lies the breathless beauty
of the uplands with moving shadows,
where kestels hover in the bright wind
and dripping crags relfect the raven's cry.

The path beside the lake
is broad and safe and groomed.
"We're getting the air," they say.

BREAKERS

Water breaks above my head,
the great grey push of it,
the curling, snarling weight
lifts, drops, flings anyhow,
throws shingle against my buried
head, sucks, drains back
above the clattering pebbles
and rears again, holds poised
for a second, as if to savour power,
crashes once more with vast momentum,
its huge muzzle crunching up the gravel.

The surf sprawls up the beach,
bubbles burst in patterns,
short respite before the next wave
plunges, lunging angrier than before.

INEVITABLE?

"Have you had flu yet?" She asked.
Why yet? Like something
in the natural order:
"have you reached 60 yet?"
or something usual like
"have you made your mince pies yet?"
even "have you made your Will yet?"
or even infrequently – "have you
served on a jury yet?"

(She might say to a skier
"have you broken your leg yet?"
or to a racing driver
"have you cracked your skull yet?")

"Oh no," I said proudly
as if I'd quite forgotten
flu existed, which I had
till then. She said
"I think I've got it."
(so glad I'd not gone in).
Her pessimism undermined
my blind morale. I took some
extra vitamins for luck.

DOMINOES

One takes a knock – gives as good as it gets
and starts a landslide. Cowardly, it does not
counter–attack the first aggressor,
rather the innocent who happens to be nearest –
knocks it for six, with unconcerned
repercussions, knocks it in the back.

They all have different faces, labelled
with varying values, but the trouble–maker
doesn't see this when he knocks them down,
their dull black backs look all the same –
same weight, same stature.

They stand by virtue of their mutual sympathy:
one slips and all the crowd are down.

OUR FLOWERS

"I like *our* flowers," he said
who'd hardly learnt to talk at all.

She was a kindly lady
praising the council flowers,
trying to bring him in,
yet his one short sentence
was dismissive – final –
spoke for all things
and all people:

our books; *our* friends; *our* hearth;
the place called home.

CLOTHING RECORD

Looking through her lavish wardrobe
"I always think of what I bought
them for, who I went out with at the time,"
she said. "Do you?"
I avoided answering, awe-inspired
and shy at such a quantity of clothes,
boy-friends galore to match.
"You can have this one if you like,"
she said. "I didn't like him much –
the friendship didn't last."
Always I felt sad for him when
I wore the pale blue dress –
the last reminder given away to me.
But that was years ago.

Now I have memories woven in different cloths,
the check dress with blue roses,
a treat when I'd been ill,
the coat that was a favourite of my son's,
the scruffy trousers worn to art class,
the wedding hats worn once,
red shoes that got too wet too soon
and never looked the same again,
the dressing gown that's darned
and patched, brought home on appro'
on the pram when all the kids were small,
skirts that saw a fashion come and go
and come again... reminders
scarcely more transient than the wearer.
Both have finite lives.

VLAMINCK

(French 20th century painter).

Where lies the secret?
Does he see differently,
discern what to leave out,
lean on a colour here,
forcing its brightness
to a higher crescendo,
subdue it there
so it dare scarcely speak?

The clouds, not much like clouds,
tear the sky open. You can hear
the clash of straw in raw sienna
thatch, feel the sludge of snow
laid on like icing. Never a boring
block of colour, graded from turquoise
to sea-green, or browns, vermilion
glowing in their heart, a tiny piece
of red, a flag high on the mast
or someone's hat.

Reflections echo in still water
seen in a dream. The trees
beside the river are enhanced
with blue, their trunks are tinged
with ginger, smell of spice.

Boats lie askew on the rough
tweed of the tide-washed beaches
where dark-clad figures battle
with the wind.

THE MEETING OF THE WATERS

Once there were three rivers
each with a valley of its own,
each with a character different
from the others.

Evan Water, mossy and serious,
peaty and deep ran through
the distant hills far out beyond the town,
a contemplative, reflecting sky
and cloud and flying waders, pondering
his long history when Covenanters
sheltered in the glens. He never
sought to enter towns, had nought
to say to people there though
to a solitary shepherd he would speak.
I never knew the Evan flood – perhaps
he was a loner without companion hillside
burns to swell the river and his banks
were steep – he was prepared for rain.

His brother Annan was a jolly river
and enjoyed the company of townsfolk,
did not resent being tamed to run through
parks with tarmac paths (why should he mind
with Tar MacAdam buried in the town).
People walked by him in their Sunday best,
children threw stones and fished for tiddlers,
courting couples strolled beside him
in the twilight. He gurgled, sang to them
and gave them flowers – the purple loosestrife,
greater willowherb with meadowsweet
and buttercups.

Often his banks were flooded as all the burns
up country fed in their contribution.
Then the gurgles rose to a great laughter
as he rushed down regardless, his grass
and flowers underwater, banks strewn
with straw and twigs, and then next day
he'd be himself again. There was humility
in his grassy banks, no sense of grandeur,
yet he had tales to tell – tales of the spa
on Hartfell's side which cured all ills,
– tales of the Devil's Beef Tub where
the border thieves had rounded up
their stolen cattle.

Their sister, Moffat Water, idled slowly
down the broad valley from St. Mary's Loch.
There was no hurry and her bed was carved
out for her years ago by snow and ice.
Wild, beautiful and spacious she was secure
in popularity, meandering on, curving
this way and that as rivers should.
In summer she was the best loved river
of the three – some came to visit Tibbie Shiels
or see the Grey Mare's Tail and didn't wait,
but many came to picnic by her banks
while white clouds touched the top
of Bodesbeck Law, the nesting curlews
bubbled in the glens and dippers flew low
over her singing stream.

Far to the north and east and west
the rivers kept themselves apart
but to the south of Moffat
they met all three together with
joyous swirls and gurglings, beaches
of pebbles in midstream with stunted
willows and banks of yellow musk.

After that Annan took the name.
Evan was pleased to leave it all
to him; he didn't crave importance,
and Moffat Water changed her name
to his who now became a river of some note
and had a town called after him
losing himself at last in vastness
in the Solway Firth.

ART MASTER

Always a teacher has a head start;
he knows his subject and you don't.
I was astonished over the years
to see uncertainty lurking beneath the mask;
gifts such as his should surely breed
assurance. The pipe and mug of coffee
gave passing comfort, but when mislaid
work ceased till they were found.

Able but unassuming, forthright and kind
he supported my indifferent talent,
tendrils holding to an established tree
whose roots were down, secure.
His nature's symphony had edge
but even the clashing notes lent colour.
Always the architecture of his mind
leaned to dynamic form, forced pictures
to speak – technique was not enough.

Scathing of trivial themes,
'kittens in baskets', yet
his strength held at the heart
a tenderness and high
regard for artists down
the ages who knew the way
to capture fire.

He was the youngest of five,
young Andy, handsome and knowing.
They'd built a special boat
for him, little, to fit,
with bright red sails
and duckboards of mahogany.
Fathers and uncles planned
a larger boat. It was half built
inside its makeshift shed,
a shed to be pulled down
when it was finished, but
before that day the island
was invaded. They sabotaged
the engines of their boats, swore
they couldn't mend them, went
hungry, foraged for limpets on the beach.

The children left for Scotland
never, as children, to see their
island home again, never to revel
in the sun–long days, the freedom
of the open sea and blown sand
on the marram grass, never to watch
green lizards on the cliff top, with gorse
smelling of coconut and crackling
in the sun, or gaze in rock pools
rich with snakelocks sea–anemones,
crabs and bullhead fish, or to go
out with nets and paddle shoes
over the popping seaweed.

When peace returned the parents welcomed
back the teenage strangers, mourning
the childhood they had not seen.

Stowed away dusty in the ancient shed
what use the little boat with faded sails?

NEW STYLE COUNTRY WALKING

Walkers are now processed, told exactly
what to see and what to think. Parking their
middle price cars in tidy rows – obedient –
they scan the map to find the 'you are here,'
and then they start. Set going like automatons
growns recount the Forestry Commission's
comments to their young. Nothing is left to chance.
Almost one expects the birds and flowers to appear
in order stating their names and place of birth.

"Have you been on the black and white house trail?
Yes, all the houses black and white. They tell
you all about how old they are and that...
(I'll take my cardy just in case – goodbye)."

"We know a picnic site where we can break our journey.
They have seats at intervals and tarmac paths
and little nooks where you can park your car –
most welcoming – they tell you where to go.
There must be lots of people: there's a carpark overflow."

For we have ceased from exploration
and the lure of the unknown is now unknown.

Or you can follow Elgar's route where
no initiative is needed on voyage
and no brave soul will venture out alone
into uncharted streets.

Or "take a summer floral walk round Cheltenham"
and see the blooms in dusty corporation rows –
another processed project. "Start at the council
offices and progress through Imperial Square,
Imperial Gardens" – if you can call it progress.

HER ROOM
(Picture by Andrew Wyeth, Rockland, Maine)

Just two sash windows
framed with shell pink curtains
their soft folds hanging
from a wire, neatly tied
about the waist to keep them trim,
simple and feminine. An old chest
stands beneath the window, plainly
fashioned, with a heart–shaped key.

A shaft of sunlight falls across
the chest, warm on the wood,
and lights upon a line of shells
ranged on the sill, and that is all.
Simplicity speaks peace in this quiet room.

A door stands open to the fields
where the blue distance stretches
into mist. I lift a shell
to listen to the murmur. It scarcely
breaks the silence with its message
from the sea.

SINCERE*

They shipped the statues in
but some were damaged
and bodged up with wax.

So they were sold, erected,
given pride of place,
vaunted, until the sun
found out the treachery
and the arms fell off,
faces became disfigured.

Honest merchants gave their
guarantee: "sincere."
They knew the searching sun
would seek out shoddy work.

Like Icarus, betrayed
when his bedraggled wings
broke loose, feeling the rush
of air through streaming hair,
remembered his father's warning
of the powerful sun.
Relentless, undiscerning,
its light and heat sought out
and purged the second-rate
– the insincere.

* *Fr. sans cire (without wax).*